UNOFFICIAL Guide
to Earning
EAGLE SCOUT

UNOFFICIAL Guide
to Earning
EAGLE SCOUT

for Parents and Scouts:
A step-by-step strategy to achieve
Scouting's highest rank

Kent Clizbe

Ashburn, Virginia, USA
wwwunofficialeagleguide.com
kent@kentclizbe.com

ISBN: 0983426457
ISBN-13: 978-0983426455

Note: All names and symbols associated with Boy Scouts of America, Eagle Scout, and related are copyrights and trademarks of the Boy Scouts of America.

Photo credits:
All digital art, photos and design are ©2014 Kent Clizbe
Except for: p. 53, Flickr: jimw

1 0 9 8 7 6 5 4 3 2

Eagle ceremony—Elias presents flag flown at overseas Army base to Isaac

DEDICATION

For all Scouts and their families.

Be prepared.

CONTENTS

Preface   i

Introduction   iii

1—Why Eagle?   1

2—Unofficial?   3

3—Scouting Outsiders   7

4—Path to Eagle—the Right Way   13

5—Biological and Psychological Facts of Life— Teen-age Boys are Brain-Damaged!   17

6—Eagle Requirements   23

7—Eagle Required Merit Badges   33

8—UNOFFICIAL Guide Strategy   39

Final Note: Cotillion   49

References   55

"First Four" Merit Badge Charts   59

UNOFFICIAL Eagle Trail Poster   155

Author Profile   161

Acknowledgements   163

PREFACE

This **UNOFFICIAL Guide to Earning Eagle** is intended for those Scouts and their families who do not have a Scouting Insider to push and pull their Scout through the organizational intricacies and bureaucratic process of earning the Eagle rank.

This book is the result of years of trial and error—of learning how *not* to do it, and how *to* do it—through the Scouting careers of two sons.

What I'd like to offer you is an **UNOFFICIAL** strategy that will put your Scout on a level playing field with Scouting Insiders. Even though you and your Scout lack their intimate knowledge of Scouting, you'll have an Insider's view—*before* you pay the price of years of hard knocks.

"On my honor I will do my best, to do my duty to God and my country…"

Kent Clizbe
Ashburn, Virginia,
March 2014

INTRODUCTION

A Boy Scout earns Eagle Rank after a long process of achievement, planning, action, and dedication.

There are many sources of information on requirements for earning the Eagle Scout rank. Nearly all are provided either by the official Boy Scouts of America (BSA) organization, or by Insiders—Troops, Councils, leaders, or others who are involved in management or leadership of Scouting.

There's never been, until now, an **UNOFFICIAL Guide to Earning Eagle**—based on experience and insights gained from being an Outsider to Scouting. This Outsider status provides a different point of view.

You may find this view a bit more rooted in the real-world of boys and their lives. You may find the tips and strategies in this **Guide** can change your Scout's life—now and for the rest of his life, since Eagle is a life-time award.

With two Eagle Scouts in the family (first son in 2006, second son in 2013), my wife and I have become intimately familiar with the process, the ups and downs, and challenges on the path to Eagle Scout. We've spent the last 14 years immersed in Scouting—immersed, but on the outside.

Because neither of us had any prior experience in Scouting, the organization and its requirements, traditions, and processes were new to us. Available information to us on the trail to Eagle was written from an Insider's perspective. The details are difficult for a Scouting Outsider to understand. Jargon-filled descriptions of requirements and processes are next to useless for Outsiders. The Scouting bureaucracy is massive and confusing, for an Outsider.

Many successful Eagle Scouts come from generations of Scouts. Their fathers were Eagles. Their fathers and mothers are active as adult leaders. These Insiders are intimately familiar with the bureaucracy and procedures of the Scouting organization. These Scouting veteran parents guide their Scouts through the trail to Eagle like an expert Indian scout guiding Lewis and Clark to the Pacific.

In the meantime, first-generation Scouts are left to the mercy of the adult leaders. These leaders, nearly always with sons in the troop, are busy. Individual attention to first-generation Scouts and parents is not always possible.

Since Scouting is made up of human beings, it's inevitable that negative human traits come up in the organization. We were not prepared for the politics of a troop. Entering Scouting with a bit of an unrealistic idealism, we were surprised to find that some parents were only involved to advance their own son. These parents, as leaders, were sometimes helpful to our boys, but were also sometimes negligent, and sometimes purposefully harmful to our boys' advancement and enjoyment in Scouting.

After 14 years of learning from the school of hard knocks, and with both boys successfully wearing their Eagle Rank, it's time to help others. The goal is to provide guidance that may make the road to Eagle less bumpy. To clarify, and simplify the process. To ensure that every boy who wants to earn Eagle has a fair chance.

With those goals in mind, I'll try to share, in this guide, details on how to best prepare yourself as a parent, and your Boy Scout for the trail to Eagle.

During our journey to Eagle with our first son, we searched for a simple guide to Scouting for Outsiders with no luck. The idea for this guide was born. But it never happened, with the crush of everyday tasks, including nurturing two Eagle-to-bes through the untidy and tumultuous teenage years.

The more we learned of the process, the more we realized that a user-friendly guide was needed for those like us, with no prior Scouting experience.

We began the Eagle-nurturing process with a mindset that echoed our approach to raising our kids. Empower him to be his own man. Encourage him to experience things on his own. Raise him to be confident, curious, independent and focused on achievement and personal growth—in short, prepare him to be a good American citizen.

> **Volunteers Required!**
> Our parenting approach may not be yours. You may prefer to be closer to your son—attend camping trips, events, etc.
> Regardless of your parenting style, please note that your Scout Troop can only function with parent volunteers.
> Please help out your troop—from setting up rooms for meetings, cleaning up after meetings, running the website, accounting, public relations, and more. All require parent volunteers.
> You could even become an Insider! And that's a good thing!

We took this approach to raising kids into the Scouting experience. We purposely did not involve ourselves in the troop. We did not go on camping trips. We did not take on leadership positions. We did assist with popcorn sales, and provided other volunteer support. But we stayed away from becoming involved in managing the troop. Our idea was that this would let our boys experience real life—where Mom and Dad were unlikely to be in charge in an organization that employed them.

As our first son rose near Eagle, it became clear that allowing him to sink or swim on his own in this process was probably not going to be successful. He was missing deadlines. He didn't understand the process. He didn't grasp the complexities of the multiple deadlines, requirements, badges, applications, communications, and other tasks required on the road to Eagle.

He loved Scouting. He loved camping. He loved the summer camps. He loved the high-adventure trips, like Philmont. He loved the camaraderie. He loved the leadership positions he held in the troop. But, like many teen-age boys, he was sloppy, not detail-oriented, unaware of the finer points of a bureaucratic process, and generally uninterested in learning about these things.

As he reached the upper levels of Scouting ranks, nearing the Eagle experience, we began to moderate our hands-off approach. We became more involved in supporting his activities. We began to work with him to plot out timelines to meet requirements. We checked on his achievements of Eagle required merit badges. He was still responsible for his activities, but we began to play a more supportive role. We became a combination of secretary and supervisor. We helped him to maintain a schedule for each project—merit badge, leadership position, right up to the Eagle project. We reminded him when things were due.

We guided him—sat down and talked about his status, and how he planned to progress.

We never did any activities for him. We provided a support structure. Luckily we made this change early enough. He was finally able to easily complete his road to Eagle when he was seventeen.

On the other hand, we observed many other first-generation Scouts fade away as they hit high school. Once their interests changed to those of a normal teenage boy—the "fumes" got them. Gas fumes from cars and girls' perfume tend to take a boy's mind off of Scouting. Many Scouts get so close to Eagle, but then never finish the final steps required. And they "age out," or turn 18 before earning Eagle.

So, armed with this experience and knowledge of boys' fundamental nature, and with a clear understanding of the Scouting bureaucracy and process, we took a very different approach with our second son. With a six year difference in age, the boys overlapped one year in the Troop before the first son left for college.

Our approach with the number two son was, in effect, the **UNOFFICIAL Guide to Earning Eagle strategy** that you'll learn here.

This guide is intended to help parents and Scouts. We recognize that the path to Eagle is a long and confusing process for first-generation Scouts. We recognize that the path is full of hurdles and roadblocks. We realize that our boys, as they enter high school, many times lose interest in Scouting, or are changing so much that they have trouble pursuing positive achievements. With these difficulties acknowledged, our tried and true methods for guiding your Scout through Eagle will make your life easier. And boys who deserve Eagle will have the chance to succeed.

An advocate for Outsiders: **The UNOFFICIAL Guide to Earning Eagle.**

CHAPTER 1   WHY EAGLE?

Why would a boy want to be an Eagle Scout? Why would parents want their boy to be an Eagle Scout? Is the concentrated, multi-year effort worth the sacrifices required? Is there a pay-off?

Let's start this book out with this claim: earning the Eagle Scout is absolutely worth the effort and sacrifice required.

Even if there was no other reward, the planning, achievement, learning, activities, and fellowship with other Scouts make the path to Eagle a reward in itself. An Eagle Scout is a step ahead of many of his non-Scout peers in the path towards fulfilling his life's meaning.

The knowledge and skills he learns from the merit badges, the leadership, the service, and his Eagle project put him head and shoulders above the vast majority of kids his age. A new Eagle Scout has built a foundation for his future success. Building on that foundation is his future.

There are external rewards, as well. The Eagle Scout rank is acknowledged and honored in the military, at many colleges, and in other civic organizations. A valued indication of a boy's potential for success in school, work, and society, Eagle Scout can be highlighted on resumes and in school applications. For the rest of his life, an Eagle Scout is part of an elite fraternity of successful achievers.

Once you've earned Eagle Scout, you hold that title for the rest of your life: "Once an Eagle, always an Eagle."

So, yes, the long and sometimes difficult path to earning Eagle Scout has its reward at the end.

As an Eagle Scout who lives with me said, "Eagle is worth it. You'll always have it. I'll always be able to say I'm an Eagle Scout. People recognize that and look up to it."

CHAPTER 2   UNOFFICIAL?

The **UNOFFICIAL Guide to Earning Eagle** is intended for Scouts and families with no prior Scouting experience. Maybe you are a father who was not a Scout. Maybe you had a brief experience, but didn't remain in Scouts. Maybe you're a mother who has never had any exposure to Scouting before. Maybe you're a relative or friend of a boy who is a Scout, or who wants to be a Scout, and you don't know anything about Scouting. Or maybe you're a boy, already a Scout, or planning to be a Scout, and you do not have any family ties to the organization.

> **Official Guide for Eagle**
> Please note that your main guides on the Path to Eagle are the official Boy Scouts of America (BSA) publications, websites, and guidance. Get to know the current Boy Scout Handbook. That is your Scout's official guidance for requirements. Additional details are on the BSA website: ***www.scouting.org***

The reason for offering an **UNOFFICIAL Guide to Earning Eagle** is because the Boy Scouts of America organization is too complicated for an Outsider to understand and decipher by yourself. The rules and regulations are complicated, confusing, and open to interpretation. For an Outsider, the organization is intimidating and confusing. Arcane rules, deep and rich culture and history, uniforms, regulations, rituals, all make it difficult for an Outsider to understand. It's like living in another country—where everything seems strange and wonderful—but confusing and frustrating. Secret handshakes, Oaths, Mottos, hand-signs, songs, traditions.

The organization is largely run by volunteers, God bless them all. It is a difficult job, by any measure. Dealing with groups of ten to eighteen year-old boys, in situations that could be dangerous, in positive and educational ways is not easy. Dealing with the boys fairly, without giving an advantage to one over another is nearly impossible, even for a saint.

The **UNOFFICIAL Guide to Earning Eagle** is your own personal Scouting Insider. We provide you with the secret tips and tricks that ease an Insider's path to Eagle. Even without being a Scouting Insider, your Scout will enjoy all the benefits they do.

CHAPTER 3   SCOUTING OUTSIDERS

My wife and I have two sons. Both sons earned their Eagle Rank—one in 2006, and the other in 2013.

Growing up, I had no experience in organized Scouting. Though I did have a subscription to Boys Life, and read it cover to cover every month in my early adolescence. I was aware of Scouting, and longed to take part in the activities I read about. But there was no one in my life who guided me to participate, and I totally missed out on the experience.

My wife grew up in another country, and had no experience with Boy Scouting at all.

Raising two boys, we realized that we needed all the help we could get to help them become productive, active, American men. Boy Scouting was the perfect adjunct to our own parental philosophy and guidance. It provided a morally-based, boy-centered, active approach to building American citizenship skills for our sons.

The Official Boy Scout Guide to Advancement says, "Boy Scouting provides a series of surmountable obstacles and steps in overcoming them through the advancement method. The Boy Scout plans his advancement and progresses at his own pace as he meets each challenge. The Boy Scout is rewarded for each achievement, which helps him gain self-confidence. The steps in the advancement system help a Boy Scout grow in self-reliance and in the ability to help others."

But this ideal of a boy advancing by himself is honored in the breach. Although there are no statistics available, personal observation of years of Scouts reveals that most boys who earn Eagle are sons of Scouting veterans. Or their parents are active adult leaders.

It seems there is value to having an "in." Like all bureaucracies, Scouting is a maze of conflicting and contradictory rules and regulations. The rules and regulations can be interpreted by different leaders in different ways at different times. Scouting's organizational goals are well-meaning. But human nature causes the system to appear arbitrary.

Scouts with fathers, mothers, or other relatives who have backgrounds in Scouting—I call them ***Scouting Insiders***—are much more likely to achieve Eagle. It's not clear why.

Are the Scouting Insiders just providing Insiders' tips to the Scouts? Or are they actively working the system for their Scouts' benefit?

In our own troop, there were several examples of Scouts who earned Eagle who probably had too much help from their parents. All of these Eagle Scouts' parents were active adult leaders in the Scouting organization. Look around your own troop. Are there un-Scout-like boys who are not checked—bad attitudes, poor Scouting spirit, and worse? Who are their parents? Committee members? Scoutmasters? Higher level adult volunteers?

The sad reality is that Scouting is a human organization. Like all human activities, you'll find examples of the dark-side of human nature. Nepotism and favoritism are a fact of life, in any human endeavor. Scouting is no different. But Scouting does provide a fair infrastructure for achievement, if you know the ins and outs.

The **Unofficial Guide** provides Scouts, and parents of Scouts, a leg up. While you cannot overcome arbitrary decisions and favoritism, you can learn the secrets to ensuring that a motivated Scout who lives the Scout Oath and Scout Law will earn Eagle.

Both our boys entered Scouting as Tiger Cubs, and stayed active until they earned their Eagles. Their Scouting experiences form a core part of who they are as young men, American citizens—a soldier and a student. I'm sure that the Scouting experience will continue to be a strong part of their lives, and will echo through the generations.

Through fourteen straight years of involvement in Scouting, with two boys becoming Eagles, we learned there was a right way to allow a boy to find his way through the process. And we learned there was a wrong way to allow a boy to find his way. We did it both ways. The right way is much more fun and rewarding.

We deliberately avoided inserting ourselves into adult leadership roles in our boys' Troop. This was precisely because of the Scouting Insider issue. Our boys had to learn to navigate the Scouting bureaucracy on their own. We only stepped in to help when they were stymied by leaders' inactions, or very rarely by bad intentions. Occasionally they ran into leaders who were deliberately obstructing the boys' progress. We helped out in those situations too. Once or twice we had to escalate issues above the Troop leadership level. But the boys were on their own during activities, conferences, camping, high adventure, and all the other parts of Scouting that challenge a boy to become a better citizen and a man.

We were active in the Troop—as "popcorn queen" and Eagle ceremony coordinator, among other support roles. But we did not become involved in any of the management roles—intentionally.

Without his parents directly involved in Troop management, the boy is empowered. He learns to communicate and to advocate for himself. He only relies on his parents when the situation is beyond his ability to solve. This is very rare. The result of this approach is boys who can stand on their own two feet. Boys who are confident and competent.

Too many times, when parents are deeply involved in Troop adult leadership—when they are Scouting Insiders—the boys' advancement becomes a "political" issue. That is, other adult leaders and volunteer members of conferences and boards allow unqualified Scouts to advance because they do not want the Scout's parents to be disappointed. This is an all too common situation, and it is unhealthy—for all concerned.

This book provides a behind-the-scenes look at a positive path to guide your Scout to life-long success, beginning with the path to Eagle.

CHAPTER 4

PATH TO EAGLE— THE RIGHT WAY

My family experienced both the right way to Eagle, and the wrong way to Eagle. This book is an attempt to help others avoid the wrong way, and move directly to the right way.

The wrong way that we discovered placed too high expectations on the boy. We expected him to remember all his deadlines. We expected him to be aware of dates, requirements, meetings, reports, and all the other massive administrative details that are part of the Scouting advancement process. We would let him fail, and then allow him to deal with the failure. We let him work with adult leaders from the Troop on scheduling and other administrative details.

This led to tremendous stress and strain. We were constantly being disappointed because our 13 year-old boy acted like a 13 year-old boy! The expectations of self-motivation were much too high. Deadlines were missed. Projects collapsed. Constant worries and arguments were the order of the day. Merit badge requirements slipped by.

The right way was much easier in the long run, though it required more direct engagement on our part. We became a sort of administrative support unit. We helped devise a calendar system to remind of deadlines. We constantly asked about requirements and projects.

Secrets to Success

We also discovered and implemented the secrets that are shared in this **UNOFFICIAL Guide to Earning Eagle**. As you'll see, the key point is front-loading the most time-consuming and arduous Eagle-required merit badges to the first months of your new Scout's career. Knocking out these requirements early makes the rest of his career seem like child's play. Except for the Eagle service project, it actually is.

The idea of being an administrative support service to your Scout is probably the most empowering approach you can take. Your Scout does all the activities and requirements himself. But you are there to keep him moving on the advancement track. You sit down with him regularly to track his progress. You use the **UNOFFICIAL Eagle** Planning Poster so he can visualize his progress.

You help him to take ownership of the process. But he always knows that you are his back-up.

That is the spirit of this **UNOFFICIAL Guide to Earning Eagle**.

Using this system, if your Scout is motivated at all, earning Eagle becomes much more likely.

Parent as Administrative Assistant

The Boy Scout journey includes a boy growing, maturing, facing challenges, overcoming challenges, learning, applying himself, having fun. The road to Eagle, as we've seen, is complicated, and probably beyond most boys' ability to achieve—on their own.

This is where his parents come in. Everything in Scouting is up to the boy. He goes in to his Scoutmaster conferences by himself. He has to tie the knots. He has to do the hiking, camping, and all the other skills required.

But his parents can provide him structure, guidance, planning, logistical support. The parents' role in the Right Way is much like an old-fashioned secretary. And that is exactly what our young Scouts need. They need help in looking at the long-term. They need help keeping focused. They need help in taking the long road to Eagle one step at a time. The **UNOFFICIAL Guide to Earning Eagle** gives both Scouts and their parents a step-by-step map to follow.

CHAPTER 5

BIOLOGICAL AND PSYCHOLOGICAL FACTS OF LIFE— TEEN-AGE BOYS ARE BRAIN-DAMAGED!

The responsibility of a boy's advancement and success is ideally left to the boy. At ten or eleven the average Boy Scout is too immature to be able to plan his advancement. At 15 or 16, boys' minds follow their hormones—thoughts of girls begin to cloud their focus. The same age brings more serious participation in sports for some boys. And many boys start thinking of driving and the freedom that will come with their driver's license. Some are even distracted by academics and the looming college decisions just a year or two away.

Besides the social pressures on boys, recent research by neuro-scientists goes so far as to describe the male adolescent brain as limited in ability to function. It's almost as if teen-age boys are brain-damaged. That realization helped my family to better manage our expectations of our growing sons. It should also form the expectations of Scouts on the path to Eagle.

> **Brain Damaged?**
>
> Brain researchers at MIT say, "The limitations of the "teen brain" [explain] why it may be difficult for teens to meet our expectations and demands for managing emotions, handling risks, responding to relationships, and engaging in complex school work or employment. In early- and mid-adolescence, the brain undergoes considerable growth and pruning, moving generally from back to front areas of the cerebral cortex."

A Monumental Task—For a Boy in a Confusing Growth Period

Earning the Eagle rank is not easy. Everyone knows that. If it was easy, all Scouts would earn it. But what makes this achievement difficult?

There are two major issues. First, the pursuit of Eagle is an effort that stretches for several years—a long-term, complicated project with multiple potential failure points. From the time a boy enters Boy Scouts, the path to Eagle can take more than six years. And these years are at the point in a boy's life that his brain and body are changing.

A boy's life, from eleven to eighteen, may be the most difficult phase of human life. He begins to experience the physical changes of puberty. The emotional changes of puberty kick in, too. And now we know that his brain is changing. It is growing, morphing. All these changes create a weird and wonderful creature—a teen-age boy.

Teen-age boys want to get out in the woods and make fires. They want to climb a mountain. They revel in the adventures and freedoms of physical activities. They love to hang around with their buddies and tell silly jokes, call each other names, and act like idiots. Scouting provides them the chance to do those things, and more.

Those teen-age boys are the raw material that will make Eagles, and American citizens. With his inability to engage in long-term thinking and planning, left to his own devices, probably not one boy in a thousand would ever earn Eagle.

The second issue that makes Eagle difficult is the complicated maze of requirements. Each requirement has several steps and sub-steps. There are inter-locking actions that must be taken in the proper sequence. Conferences, planning, outreach, activities. Boys want to get out in the woods and make fires. All of these administrative actions aren't natural or easy for boys.

Even if a boy is focused and capable of long-term thinking and planning, the maze of requirements is confusing. It is a complex administrative task. It is confusing, even for adults.

So, now we understand the complexity. And we understand that teen-age boys are just not designed to handle the long-term thinking, planning, and administration required to be successful in this task.

Regardless of why, boys ten to seventeen years-old are uniquely poorly suited mentally for the focus and dedication that is required to plan a path to earning Eagle.

That is, if they are left to do it alone.

This is so important, let me repeat it: (Most) ***boys 10 to 17 years-old are unable to earn Eagle on their own.***

While it would be perfect if our Scouts could all independently plan and carry out a path to Eagle, the nature of young boys makes that extremely unlikely. So, a main part of the **UNOFFICIAL** path is the Scout's parents providing support and guidance.

Exception Proves the Rule

I've closely observed the advancement paths of a dozen or more Eagle Scouts, from Tenderfoot to their Eagle Court of Honor. I attended Troop meetings as often as possible. These boys were close friends of my sons. We hosted them for birthday parties. We drove them to Scouting events. I worked on their Eagle projects.

That number includes my own two Eagle Scout sons. This group of boys may not be exactly representative of all Boy Scouts. But they are surely a good cross section. Of that group, there was only boy who earned Eagle on nearly total self-motivation.

He was a special case, though. Both his mother and father were active in the Troop, from the day he crossed over from Webelos, where his Dad was his Den Leader. A couple of years into his Scouting career, his parents divorced. His dad remained active in the Troop.

When the boy was thirteen or fourteen, his dad died unexpectedly. The boy was left pretty much on his own in Scouting. He became even more active than before. He was elected Senior Patrol Leader, and then re-elected a couple of times. He completed his Eagle project, all the requirements, and earned Eagle at fifteen. He was a Scouting dynamo— total motivation and Scout spirit. This Eagle Scout, evidently motivated by a desire to make his late father proud, is the exception that proves the rule.

The rest of the Scouts I've seen reach Eagle were typical teen-age boys. They moped and clowned. They played and worked. They mostly lacked driving motivation. But most of them were guided by their Scouting Insider parents. Without the motivation, help, pushing, and guidance coming from their (mostly) Insider parents, it's likely that the path to Eagle for these boys would have been much more difficult.

CHAPTER 6   EAGLE REQUIREMENTS

The specific requirements for earning the Eagle rank can change over time. So, we won't go into great detail, just the basics. The basic set of requirements will stay the same.

> **BSA Website**
> For current requirements, see the official BSA website.
> ***www.scouting.org***

From decade to decade, specific merit badges may change—some are added, some dropped, some substitutions are made. But the basic set of requirements will likely remain the same.

Basic Requirements

☐ Earn Life Scout Rank.

☐ Be active in your Troop for six months as a Life Scout.

☐ Demonstrate that you follow the Scout Oath and the Scout Law in your daily life.

☐ Provide references to confirm that you follow the Oath and Law—parents, teachers, religious leaders, coaches, employers, or others.

☐ Complete a minimum number of merit badges total in your Scouting career (in 2014, the number is 21).

☐ Complete all the Eagle-required merit badges (in 2014 there are 13).

☐ As a Life Scout, serve at least six months in a position of responsibility.

☐ As a Life Scout, plan and complete a service project—the Eagle Project.

☐ Complete an Eagle Rank Scoutmaster conference.

☐ Complete a statement of your ambitions and life purpose.

☐ Complete an Eagle Rank Board of Review.

As you can see, achieving Life Scout is the first goal of a new Scout who aspires to Eagle. This achievement requires that he progress through the ranks—Tenderfoot, Second Class, First Class, and Star—that come before Life.

12 Steps to Eagle List
This website provides the Insider's view of the official steps required for a Scout to move from Life to Eagle:
http://meritbadge.org/wiki/index.php/12_Steps_From_Life_to_Eagle

Many troops make an effort to guide new Scouts to reach their First Class rank in their first year of Scouting. This is an excellent foundation to build a path toward Eagle. If your troop is not in the "First Class in the first year" mode, then you can take that as your own goal—your Scout will earn First Class in one year.

Subjective Requirements—Living the Scout Oath and Law

When your Scout earns his Life rank, it's a good time for a heart-to-heart talk. He is now very close to Eagle. He will need to focus and concentrate his efforts towards earning Eagle.

A couple of key requirements that are worth talking about in this heart-to-heart are the very subjective requirements: Demonstrate that you follow the Scout Oath and the Scout Law in your daily life; and references who will confirm that you follow the Oath and Law— parents, teachers, religious leaders, coaches, employers, or others.

With his changing brain, hormones, and interests, your Scout may be in a developmental period that includes a bad attitude. This can be a problem on the path to Eagle (not to mention at home!). Normal developing boys get in trouble. Sometimes they have a "smart mouth." Sometimes they come across as being unpleasant.

All of these behaviors and attitudes are pretty much against the Law and Oath. It is very likely that any Scout, during his time of development, will make a bad impression on someone, or maybe on lots of other people. For one thing, the fact that most boys are natural violators of the Law and Oath is a fantastic confirmation of how important the Law and Oath are in helping our boys develop into good citizens and men. However, your Scout now needs to start building some good relationships with others, consciously demonstrating his dedication to the Oath and the Law.

Your Scout should start talking to the adults who he intends to ask for references. Bringing up the subject in advance and asking the references for their impressions or advice could be very helpful. Any potential references who are not willing, or who share bad impressions, may not be suitable for use in the actual application. However, your Scout should use the input these pre-reference interviews provide to adjust his attitude, and his adherence to the Oath and Law. A bad word a year and a half before the Eagle Board of Review gives your Scout plenty of time to get right with the Oath and Law.

"Active" and Leadership

These two requirements are likely the easiest to meet. If your Scout goes to every Troop meeting, and goes on Troop camping trips and other activities, he is "active."

However, if your Scout has developed other interests, which is more likely if he is past 14 or so, he may not be making all the Troop meetings. He may be missing camping trips. The "Active" requirement becomes a bit more problematic. There is not an exact measurement of "Active in the Troop." The best approach is for your Scout to attend all Troop meetings. If there's any confusion about what active means, be sure your Scout speaks to Troop adult leadership now—don't wait until the Eagle Scoutmaster conference to learn that your Scout doesn't meet this requirement.

At the same time, the Leadership requirement is easier to define. However, there are some gray areas. There are many positions in the Troop that can meet this requirement. The positions do not have to be elected Leader positions. Instead of "Leadership" Scouts can serve in "positions of responsibility" instead. It's important for your Scout to work with the Troop's boy leaders and adult leaders to ensure that your Scout is in a

> **Positions of Responsibility**
> Troop guide, Order of the Arrow troop representative, Den Chief, Scribe, Librarian, Historian, Quartermaster, Junior Assistant Scoutmaster, Chaplain Aide, Instructor, Webmaster, Leave No Trace trainer.

Leadership position, or position of responsibility soon after earning Life.

If your Scout takes on a Leadership position, and attends every Troop meeting, these requirements are simple to attain.

Service Project Requirement

Of course, the "Eagle Project" is what most people associate with the Eagle rank. It is an important part of the requirements, but probably not the part that derails most Scouts who don't make Eagle.

There are many resources available to guide Scout's through the Eagle Project.

> **UNOFFICIAL Tip**
> Eagle projects require massive amounts of administrative details—planning, scheduling, communications with volunteers, writing the final project report.
> Your Scout needs administrative support. Let him be the "boss," and you are his assistant. Remind him of deadlines, emails to send, appointments to make and keep, reports to write. Guide him through to a successful completion.

While it is complicated, and requires a large effort, the Troop and BSA provide support in many ways. Look on the BSA website *www.scouting.org*. Another excellent resource is *www.meritbadge.org*, an independent website run by Scouting Insiders.

But the most important resource, that your Troop will provide your Scout, is the official Eagle Scout Service Project Workbook. It is the written record of all your Scout's activities for the Project.

The most common downfall of aspiring Eagles, with the project, is failure to complete the final written report. It's a hard deadline to keep, and it is required.

> **Eagle Project Checklist**
>
> A useful checklist for your Scout's project:
> **http://meritbadge.org/wi ki/images/f/f1/Eagle_Proje ct_Plan_Checklist.pdf**

A couple of things to keep in mind—as your Scout should be planning for this project far in advance—he should take part in every Eagle project other Scouts do in his Troop. He should learn from his fellow-Scouts' successes and mistakes. Participating in others' projects is also a great show of Scouting spirit, and can count for service hours. An all around win-win.

Some things your Scout should think about early in his Scouting career, anticipating his Eagle project are:

Potential beneficiaries: These must be non-Scouting-related organizations. Schools, religious institutions, community organizations, or other non-Scouting groups can all receive the benefits of an Eagle project.

Volunteers: Eagle projects must be carried out with volunteer labor. Recruiting and organizing the volunteers is a big part of the project. The sooner your Scout starts talking to potential volunteers, the better. Your Scout can recruit from his church or religious group, his non-Scout school friends, family, the Troop, other Scout groups, the community, and more.

Materials: Depending on the project, your Scout may need to solicit donations of materials from businesses, or money to pay for materials. While it may be too early, before you know exactly what the project is, your Scout could begin to build relationships with hardware stores, or other businesses.

Project Report: The final report, usually contained in the official Eagle Scout Service Project Workbook, will require your Scout to provide details on these issues (see meritbadge.org for full details):

- *What was the project?*

- *How did it benefit others?*

- *Who from the group benefiting from the project gave guidance?*

- *Who helped carry out the project?*

- *What materials were used and how were they acquired?*

- *Did the candidate demonstrate leadership of others?*

- *Did he indeed direct the project rather than do all the work himself?*

- *Was the project of real value to the religious institution, school, or community group?*

- *Who from the group benefiting from the project may be contacted to verify the value of the project?*

- *Did the project follow the approved plan or were modifications needed to bring it to its completion?*

The sooner your Scout knows that he'll have to answer these questions, the sooner he can start thinking about, and planning for, the project and the report.

Eagle Project Ideas
A useful brain-storming resource—prior Eagle projects:
http://www.scoutorama.com/project/

CHAPTER 7   EAGLE REQUIRED MERIT BADGES

The list of Eagle-required merit badges has changed through the years. The following list is current in 2014. Be sure that you check with your Troop and the official BSA Handbook for your Scout's requirements. The idea behind the Eagle-required merit badges list is to provide a common body of skills and knowledge that all Eagles must master. The skills gained while earning these badges provide an excellent background for being a productive American citizen.

Eagle-Required Merit Badges

First Aid

Citizenship in the Community

Citizenship in the Nation

Citizenship in the World

Communications

Personal Fitness

Emergency Preparedness or *Lifesaving*

Environmental Science

Personal Management

Swimming, Hiking or *Cycling*

Camping

Family Life

All of these badges require significant effort and focus. The subjects they cover are the core of Scouting—that's why they're Eagle-required! As we will discuss in the **UNOFFICIAL Strategy** chapter, you must complete these badges as soon as possible.

These merit badges naturally fall into categories. When you think of them in these categories, the strategy for early completion becomes more clear.

Category: Merit Badges Earned in the Classroom

In many Troops, some of the Eagle-required badges are completed in "Merit Badge Classes." Many Troops have active merit badge activities, led by merit badge counselors.

The "Citizenship" group of Eagle-required badges—Community, Nation, and World—lend themselves well to completing most activities in a class or at home. These badges can be completed by most Scouts with less effort than many other categories.

Another common "Classroom" category badge is First Aid. The required learning and practice can be done during Troop meetings, or before or after meetings. Or even in a special class time outside Troop meetings. Communications is also commonly offered in Troop classes.

If your Troop does not offer classes for these badges, you may want to suggest they do. Or you could volunteer to be the counselor for these, and set up the classes yourself.

Category: Summer Camp Merit Badges

Some merit badges are much easier to earn during a Boy Scout summer camp. The intensive daily learning sessions, physical facilities, and Scout focus are helpful in completing these badges: Lifesaving, Swimming, Emergency Preparedness, and Environmental Science.

Part of the **UNOFFICIAL Guide Strategy** is to attend as many summer camps as possible, in the early years of a Scout's career. At summer camp, be sure that your Scout signs up to earn these Eagle-required badges. And if there are others offered, be sure to put those Eagle-required badges at the top of the list for his summer camp activities.

Category: "First Four"

Family Life, Personal Management, Personal Fitness, and Camping are the most time-consuming and intensive merit badges of all the Eagle-required badges.

These four Eagle-required merit badges all require long-term projects, or data collection. The projects usually require the Scout to keep track of an activity or other personal data—like household chore completion. Other activities in these four badges are sometimes offered in classes by Troops. But the individual record-keeping, tracking progress over a month to three months, must be done by the Scout at home.

Because of the intensive record-keeping requirement for these badges, many Scouts shy away from even beginning these badges. For most Scouts, it's not fun and easy to plan out a personal fitness journal, and then keep track of your times and progress on a chart.

> **Details on First Four**
> *Personal Fitness:*
> http://meritbadge.org/wiki/index.php/Personal_Fitness
> *Personal Management:*
> http://meritbadge.org/wiki/index.php/Personal_Management
> *Family Life:*
> http://meritbadge.org/wiki/index.php/Family_Life
> *Camping:*
> http://meritbadge.org/wiki/index.php/Camping

The difficulty of the charting and record-keeping in these badges makes them, many times, the barrier that Scouts do not clear in their path toward Eagle.

Our experience led us to focus the **UNOFFICIAL Guide Strategy** on earning these First Four as the most important single thing your Scout can do in the path to Eagle. Your Scout should start on these badges immediately.

Charts and Checklists

In the appendices at the end of this book, you'll find charts and checklists to help your Scout in the First Four record-keeping. We've produced a useful visual aid, in the form of the **UNOFFICIAL Eagle** Planning Poster that you can use to keep your Scout on track toward Eagle. A small version is also provided in the appendices. You can order a more useful wall-sized version at the link provided with the version in this book.

Other Merit Badges

In addition to the 13 Eagle-required merit badges, a Scout must earn a total of 21 merit badges. That is, he must earn eight more merit badges besides his 13 Eagle-required badges.

Many Troops conduct Merit badge days, or indoor overnight events in which Scouts can earn a couple, or more badges, or at least complete a good portion of a badge's requirements.

Boy Scout summer camps are also excellent for earning merit badges. Most summer camps offer intensive sessions designed to complete the requirements for several badges in a week or two.

Many troops also offer merit badge classes, depending on their counselor availability, for a variety of badges. Your Scout should participate in these whenever he can.

By taking advantage of the organized activities, and summer camps, your Scout should earn more than enough merit badges to meet the minimum Eagle requirements.

Confusing Requirement

The Official Eagle Requirements list includes a confusing note in parentheses: "Earn a total of 21 merit badges (10 more than you already have)…"

What they mean is: "If you have earned only the minimum merit badges up to your achieving Life Scout, you will need to earn 10 more."

There is *no* requirement that the Scout must earn 10 merit badges while he is a Life Scout. The total number of merit badge required for Eagle is 21.

If a Scout had earned all 13 Eagle-required merit badges and 8 other merit badges before he became a Life Scout, then he *does not* need to earn any more. Of course earning more badges does not hurt, and is fun and interesting.

CHAPTER 8
UNOFFICIAL GUIDE STRATEGY

As boys develop physically, mentally, emotionally and socially, there is only a short window of opportunity when we can reach them and help them focus on achievement. Before their hormones begin to crank up, and distract them from non-girl interests, they have only a couple of years in Scouting. They don't know that their most productive Scouting days are numbered. But you and I do. And your job, as your Scout's administrative assistant, is to encourage him to make the most of those early years.

Timing: Eleven to Thirteen—Key Years

From eleven to thirteen are the key years—the first two years of Scouting. During these two years, most boys are also more likely to be receptive to parental guidance and suggestions. The early teen-age years, after thirteen through eighteen are very likely to be trying times. Emotional, physical, psychological, and social development are painful for many boys.

So, as your Scout's motivating force, use this period (11 to 13 years old) when your Scout is able to think straight, and is interested and cooperative, to work with him. He should earn as many of the Eagle-required merit badges as possible in this period.

Now that you understand why it is so crucial for your Scout to achieve early in his Scouting career, let's introduce the key elements of the **UNOFFICIAL Strategy**

Following these strategic points will improve the chance that your Scout will earn Eagle. This is not a guarantee, but this Outsider approach will give your Scout the Insider's chance of making his Eagle.

Review these points, consider them, and work on applying them. Some of the points may not be perfectly clear at first. For example, the "bypass blockages" may not make sense, until you bump up against a blockage. You may want to review the key points once a year, or so, and be sure that you're keeping on track.

They are presented in priority order. The first Strategy Key Point is the most important—providing administrative assistance to your Scout. The second is the next most important—ensuring that your Scout starts immediately on the First Four merit badges. And so on, down to the sixth. If you can put in practice all of these Strategic Key Points, it is likely that your Scout will reach his goal.

UNOFFICIAL Strategy Key Points:

1. Parent as administrative assistant

2. First Four merit badges

3. Be ready to bypass blockages

4. Summer camps

5. Camping trips

6. Participate in other Scouts' Eagle projects

> **Unofficial Tip: Scout Binder**
> Create a binder to use for storing and organizing scouting achievements. The main feature of this binder is about 10 clear plastic sheets—commonly used to display baseball cards. Store all your Scout's merit badge cards in this binder. When it is time to review all achievements at the Eagle Scoutmaster conference, the Scout just takes his binder to the meeting. It's also handy to keep papers, certificates, and other Scouting records, all in one place.

UNOFFICIAL Strategy Key Point 1

Parent as administrative assistant

The Boy Scout journey includes a boy growing, maturing, facing challenges, overcoming challenges, learning, applying himself, and having fun. The road to Eagle, as we've seen, is complicated, and probably beyond most boys' ability to achieve—on their own.

This is where his parents come in. Everything in Scouting is up to the boy. He goes in to his Scoutmaster conferences by himself. He has to tie the knots. He has to do the hiking, camping, building shelter, and all the other skills required.

But his parents can provide him structure, guidance, planning, logistical support. And that is exactly what our young Scouts need. They need help in looking at the long-term. They need help keeping focused. They need help in taking the long road to Eagle one step at a time. Parents, grand-parents, uncles and aunts, big brothers and sisters, and other concerned adults can provide the structure and long-term planning and support that our Scouts need.

We cannot do the activities for our Scouts. But we can help our Scouts plan. We can remind Scouts of deadlines. We can help our Scouts plot out their schedules. We can provide rides to meetings, be sure our Scouts get there on time. Our role is to be an assistant to our Scout on this long journey to Eagle.

UNOFFICIAL Strategy Key Point 2

Start the "First Four" Eagle-required merit badges now!

To ensure future success, your Scout should complete the First Four Eagle-required merit badges—Personal Fitness, Personal Management, Family Life, and Camping (see Chapter 6—Eagle Requirements for details on the First Four). These all include long-term projects or record-keeping. Begin working on the First Four Eagle-required badges as soon as you join your Troop.

Many Troops have intensive programs that lead new Scouts to earning their First Class rank in their first year of Scouting. Many of these programs offer structured activities (personal fitness tests, for example) that are part of the First Four Eagle-required merit badges.

Be sure that your Scout takes part in those activities. The sooner that your Scout begins the long-term, record-keeping requirements of the First Four, the sooner he can complete them. See the charts and guides in the back of this book—these will make the record-keeping easier for each of the First Four.

UNOFFICIAL Strategy Key Point 3
Be ready to bypass blockages

As mentioned earlier, Scouting Insiders are many times the source of conflict for families who are not linked in to the organization.

Unfortunately, some of these Scouting Insiders not only work the system for their own Scout's benefit. They also have been known to actively inhibit other Scouts' advancement. This sounds incredible, but it is true. One Scouting Insider volunteered to be the merit badge counselor for an Eagle-required merit badge. Ten boys had joined the Troop together and were progressing together. The plan was for the group of Scouts to earn the Eagle-required badge over the summer. Besides summer camps, the Troop had nearly no planned activities that summer.

The Scouting Insider, whose son was in the group working on the badge, provided his email address to the group after meeting in person one time. After that, other boys in the group tried to set up personal meetings—badge requirements included meeting with the counselor. The Scouting Insider ignored the emails for a few weeks. Finally he answered the emails, saying that he was traveling for work; check again in a couple more weeks. This continued the entire summer. Of the ten boys who started the badge work in the spring, only one Scout was awarded the Eagle-required badge at the first Court of Honor the next Fall. That Scout was the son of the Scouting Insider.

While it would be generous and kind to interpret this as a failing of the other Scouts, it would not be true. Clearly this Scouting Insider felt that his son was in competition with the other Scouts. Instead of urging his son to do well, and guiding him along the righteous path, this Scouting Insider instead chose to make his son look better by sabotaging other Scouts' efforts to earn the Eagle-required badge.

This is an example of a misuse of power by a Scouting Insider. It would be great to say that this is uncommon. But that would not be accurate.

The positive side of this experience is that Scouts who had to deal with this experience are better prepared for the real world. There are many negative people in any organization— work, school, social, or professional. Learning to deal with people like this is a good life lesson.

> **UNOFFICIAL Tip**
> A formal appeal process is available to Scouts who believe that official Scouting decisions were unfair or not warranted.
> Details can be found in the BSA's Official Guide to Advancement:
> *http://www.scouting.org/filestore/pdf/33088.pdf*

However, in that group of ten Scouts, nine did not earn that Eagle-required merit badge that summer. The Scouting Insider's son, who did earn the badge, went on to earn Eagle. How many of the other nine Scouts became discouraged, and gave up? How many were permanently set back in their advancement? We don't have the details on what happened to all of those nine. We do know that one of those nine had parents who used the **Unofficial Guide** techniques. He went on to earn his Eagle.

The **UNOFFICIAL Strategy** point is that you must be aware of this Insider tendency. And you also must be aware that there are official channels, above your Troop, which are generally more fair and more focused on benefits for the entire Scouting organization.

Find the details of your troop, district, council, National Boy Scout Committee online, or from a Troop adult leader. The higher up the appeal process your issue goes, the more likely you are to find unbiased decisions.

UNOFFICIAL Strategy Key Point 4

Summer camps

One of the most enjoyable experiences for boys in Scouting is the one or two week Scouting summer camp. Various Scouting bodies offer summer camps—in the mountains, by the sea, on lakes, or other natural settings. These camps usually provide intensive sessions designed to allow Scouts to earn merit badges—some Eagle-required. Even if the badges are not Eagle-required, there is still the requirement to earn merit badges for each rank advancement, and the total badge requirement, as well.

Besides having a fantastic summer experience, growing in independence and self-reliance, having fun, being active, and meeting new people, summer camps can provide Scouts with a good chunk of their merit badge requirements.

Use your Scout's early years in the program to hit these camps. Before he has conflicting interests, and while he is young and enthusiastic, summer camps provide a lifelong memory, and excellent Eagle advancement opportunities. Use them in your Scout's path to Eagle.

UNOFFICIAL Strategy Key Point 5

Camping trips

The Camping merit badge is one of the First Four. It requires 20 nights of sleeping "under the stars" or in a tent the scout erected himself. Many Troops go camping once a month in the spring and fall, usually on weekends.

At two nights for each weekend camping trip, that would require 10 solid months of camping. It's more likely that your Scout will be free for weekend camping trips at a younger age, before he has other activities and distractions on the weekends. Back to a familiar refrain, knock out the camping night requirement as soon as possible, before he has too many scheduling conflicts.

Your family may have to make some sacrifices during your Scout's first couple of years, when he is camping regularly. Surely there will be conflicts with family trips, vacations, or other events. If your Scout is motivated, and wants Eagle, and you support him, then you'll be able to work around his camping trips.

Many promising Scouts have lost their chance to earn Eagle when they joined a "travel" soccer team at 11 or 12, before completing 20 nights camping. A good rule of thumb for prioritizing activities—will your son's soccer season (or fill in the blank with any other competing activity) have any bearing on his life in 20 years? Then compare that with the potential of earning Eagle Scout, and the meaning for the rest of his life.

UNOFFICIAL Strategy Key Point 6

Other Scouts' Eagle projects

The final Strategic Point will make your Scout's own Eagle project less challenging and mysterious. As soon as he joins his Troop, he should begin participating in Troop members' Eagle projects. And you should too. Your Scout may just be extra hands (some projects require skills and muscle that 11 year-olds lack), but he'll never be turned away.

He (and you) will have the chance to observe how the Eagle Scout candidate organizes and supervises the project. You'll see what role the parents and adult Troop leaders play in the project. As your Scout gets closer to his own Eagle project, it's likely that some Scouts close to him in age and rank will be doing their projects. He can volunteer to be an assistant at his buddies' projects, and he'll get an even better idea what is required.

After working on Eagle projects for a couple of years, your Scout will be much more comfortable with the idea of doing his own. And his willing participation in Eagle projects will be noticed by the Troop, adding to his Scout spirit standing, and his reputation for living the Oath and Law. All of this will make it easier for him to recruit the volunteers needed for his own up-coming Eagle project.

FINAL NOTE: COTILLION

The Boy Scouts' Eagle Scout program is a time-tested way to develop boys into good and productive citizens. The skills and knowledge that a boy develops while becoming an Eagle touch on all parts of his personal development and his life in the community.

The genius of the requirements is how complete they are. First Aid, Citizenship in the World, Citizenship in the Community, Family Life, Swimming, and the other Eagle merit badges each represent a segment of life. Putting them all together, you see that all the most important segments of life are there.

Except one.

The Boy Scouts activities are all focused on boys being boys. The Eagle requirements are focused on turning those boys into good men, and good citizens. The activities and meetings are all-boy-all-the-time. This can be a bit crazy, and like a zoo. But that's how boys are.

Overall the focus can be seen as too much on the "boy" part. In fact, many boys drop out of Scouts when they become interested in girls. A boy can complete the entire Eagle program without ever coming into contact with a girl. Even Eagle Scouts can be quite rough around the edges in social situations.

This is a major deficiency in a program designed to cultivate a boy to manhood and responsible citizenship.

Relations between males and females, whether social, professional, or romantic, can be the most important and rewarding of a man's life. They are definitely the most difficult,

for most men, to master. But Scouting completely ignores this fundamentally important area of a young man's life.

The Scouting program's focus on the boy does not need to change. It just needs an addition.

This is why, for the sake of the full social development of boys, we supplemented our Eagle's developmental program with a program that focused on social skills, especially in dealing with girls.

National League of Junior Cotillion

The best social program in the country, and probably the world, is a program known as Cotillion. This program provides a chance for young men and women (the main program runs from fifth grade through eighth grade, the early years of a boy's Scouting career) to learn how to socialize.

> **UNOFFICIAL Tip**
> To find the Cotillion program in your area, see the NLJC's website:
> *http://www.nljc.com/*

A Cotillion Director described her program goals as, "… preparing these young men to face future social situations, college recruiters, internship coordinators, and employers, with increased skills, confidence and integrity.   Simply put, it means knowing the kind and correct thing to do in any social situation and then actually following through!"

The boys and girls mix together in a controlled, formal setting. Boys learn to respect girls as human beings, and as friends. They participate in etiquette lessons, dancing lessons, and learn other social skills. They take part in social outings—square dance, river cruises, formal dinners, and more.

The formal dances are as much of a help as all of the lessons. A dance teacher leads them through all the steps of ballroom dancing. But that is not the actual point of the lesson—although they learn ballroom dancing, the actual value of the activity is the boys' extended proximity to girls. And the boys must respectfully interact with the girls. The boys hold hands with the girls. They put their hands in the proper position on the girl's waist and shoulders. All of this proximity helps boy become used to being near girls. After a few sessions, most boys begin to relax and enjoy the experience.

Combined with the lessons learned as an Eagle, Cotillion training is a requirement that polishes up the rough edges. With those smooth edges, a boy is all ready to become a completely well-rounded American man.

I give Cotillion the highest recommendation possible for parents who want to supplement Boy Scouts, sports, and academics with a guide for their son's socialization. It is a proven program. The results are impressive and life-changing.

There are even Cotillion programs for younger boys (kindergarten to fourth grade). And there is a high school program—the high school events focus more on socializing than on learning. Cotillion also offers

crash courses for boys who are not able to attend regularly, at any age.
Please consider Cotillion for your son.

REFERENCES

BSA Official Eagle Scout Fact Sheet

http://www.scouting.org/About/FactSheets/EagleScouts.aspx

BSA Official Requirements Book

http://meritbadge.org/wiki/index.php/Boy_Scout_Requirements

BSA Official Guide to Advancement—Eagle Rank

http://www.scouting.org/scoutsource/guidetoadvancement/eaglescoutrank.aspx

BSA Official Guide to Advancement—Boards of Review

http://www.scouting.org/scoutsource/GuideToAdvancement/BoardsofReview.aspx

BSA Official Guide—Advancement Resources

http://www.scouting.org/scoutsource/BoyScouts/AdvancementandAwards/resources.aspx

BSA Official Guide—Advancement and Awards

http://www.scouting.org/scoutsource/BoyScouts/AdvancementandAwards.aspx

US Scouts Guide—Eagle Requirements

http://www.usscouts.org/advance/boyscout/bsrank7.asp

MeritBadge.org Requirements for Eagle

http://meritbadge.org/wiki/index.php/Eagle_Scout_Rank

Merit Badge Worksheets

http://meritbadge.org/wiki/index.php/Merit_Badge_Worksheets

Eagle Project Ideas

http://www.scoutorama.com/project/

Eagle Project Checklist

http://meritbadge.org/wiki/images/f/f1/Eagle_Project_Plan_Checklist.pdf

National Eagle Scouts Association

http://www.nesa.org/

History of Eagle

http://scoutingmagazine.org/issues/0211/d-wwas.html

Evolution of Eagle Rank Requirements

http://www.troop97.net/bsaeagle.htm

Boys' Teen Brain

http://journeytomanhood.blogspot.com/2008/08/that-frustrating-teen-brain.html

Man-Making

http://journeytomanhood.blogspot.com/

MIT Young Adult Development Project—Teen Brain

http://hrweb.mit.edu/worklife/youngadult/brain.html#adolescence

"FIRST FOUR" MERIT BADGE CHARTS

The charts in this section are provided to help your Scout complete the requirements for the all-important First Four Eagle-required merit badges.

The charts (and a small version of the UNOFFICIAL Eagle Planning Poster) are available in a magazine format at a discount for book owners. Forward proof of purchase in an email to: *chartsplease@unofficialeagleguide.com*

Or, to purchase the magazine alone, see the website: **www.unofficialeagleguide.com**

Personal Fitness Merit Badge

12 week Fitness Program requirement:

Complete the aerobic fitness, flexibility, muscular strength, and body composition tests. Record your results in the charts provided on the following pages.

1. Use the *Pre-Fitness Test* chart to record your first fitness test.

2. Use one chart (*12 week Fitness Program Log*) each week to record your times and results. Each week use the blanks to record:

   - Week Number of your program
   - Scout Name
   - Date

3. Use the *Post-Program Fitness Test* chart to record your results of the Fitness test after your 12 week program.

Personal Fitness Merit Badge

Fitness Test Charts

Pre-Fitness Test

Scout Name:_____ **Date:**_____

Test ⇒	Aerobic Fitness	Flexibility	Strength
Run/Walk **Time** *to complete 1 mile*			
Sit-n-reach box **4th reach** *distance Hold for 15 sec.*			
Sit-ups *Number correctly done in 60 sec.*			
Pull-ups *Number correctly done in 60 sec.*			
Push-ups *Number correctly done in 60 sec.*			

Personal Fitness Merit Badge

12-Week Fitness Program Log

Weekly Fitness Activity Log: Week Number _____

Scout Name: _____   **Date:** _____

Personal Fitness Merit Badge

Order book and poster: unofficialeagleguide.com c2014 Kent Clizbe

	Run, Swim, Bike	Exercise name _____	Exercise name _____	Exercise name _____	Heart rate
Distance/Time					
Number of repetitions	▨				▨
Beats per minute before/after	▨	▨	▨	▨	
Other/Notes					

Personal Fitness Merit Badge

12-Week Fitness Program Log

Weekly Fitness Activity Log: Week Number _____

Scout Name: _____   **Date:** _____

Personal Fitness Merit Badge

	Run, Swim, Bike	Exercise name ___	Exercise name ___	Exercise name ___	Heart rate
Distance/Time					
Number of repetitions					
Beats per minute before/after					
Other/Notes					

Order book and poster: unofficialeagleguide.com ©2014 Kent Clizbe

Personal Fitness Merit Badge

12-Week Fitness Program Log

Weekly Fitness Activity Log: Week Number _____

Scout Name: _____ **Date:** _____

	..., Swim, Bike	Exercise name _____	Exercise name _____	Exercise name _____	Heart rate
Distance/Time					
Number of repetitions					
Beats per minute before/after					
Other/Notes					

Order book and poster: unofficialeagleguide.com c2014 Kent Clizbe

Personal Fitness Merit Badge

Personal Fitness Merit Badge

12-Week Fitness Program Log

Weekly Fitness Activity Log: Week Number_____

Scout Name:_____   **Date:_____**

Personal Fitness Merit Badge

	Run, Swim, Bike	Exercise name _____	Exercise name _____	Exercise name _____	Heart rate
Dis, .e/Time		▓▓▓	▓▓▓	▓▓▓	▓▓▓
Number of repetitions	▓▓▓				▓▓▓
Beats per minute before/after	▓▓▓	▓▓▓	▓▓▓	▓▓▓	
Other/Notes					

Personal Fitness Merit Badge

12-Week Fitness Program Log

Weekly Fitness Activity Log: Week Number _____

Scout Name: _____ **Date:** _____

Personal Fitness Merit Badge

	Run, Swim, Bike	Exercise name ___	Exercise name ___	Exercise name ___	Heart rate
Distance/Time					
Number of repetitions					
Beats per minute before/after					
Other/Notes					

Order book and poster: unofficialeagleguide.com ©2014 Kent Clizbe

Personal Fitness Merit Badge

12-Week Fitness Program Log

Weekly Fitness Activity Log: Week Number _____

Scout Name: _____   **Date:** _____

Personal Fitness Merit Badge

Order book and poster:
unofficialeagleguide.com
©2014 Kent Clizbe

	Run, Swim, Bike	Exercise name ____	Exercise name ____	Exercise name ____	Heart rate
Distance, time					
Number of repetitions					
Beats per minute before/after					
Other/Notes					

Personal Fitness Merit Badge

12-Week Fitness Program Log

Weekly Fitness Activity Log: Week Number _____

Scout Name: _____   **Date:** _____   *Personal Fitness Merit Badge*

	Run, Swim, Bike	Exercise name ____	Exercise name ____	Exercise name ____	Heart rate
Distance/Time					
Number of repetitions					
Beats per minute before/after					
Other/Notes					

Order book and poster: unofficialeagleguide.com ©2014 Kent Clizbe

Personal Fitness Merit Badge

12-Week Fitness Program Log

Weekly Fitness Activity Log: Week Number _____

Scout Name: _____   **Date:** _____

Personal Fitness Merit Badge

	Run, Swim, Bike	Exercise name ____	Exercise name ____	Exercise name ____	Heart rate
Distance/Time					
Number of repetitions					
Beats per minute before/after					
Other/Notes					

Personal Fitness Merit Badge

12-Week Fitness Program Log

Weekly Fitness Activity Log: Week Number _____

Scout Name: _____   **Date:** _____

Personal Fitness Merit Badge

	Run, Swim, Bike	Exercise name _____	Exercise name _____	Exercise name _____	Heart rate
Distance/Time		▓▓▓	▓▓▓	▓▓▓	
Number of repetitions	▓▓▓				▓▓▓
Beats per minute before/after	▓▓▓	▓▓▓	▓▓▓	▓▓▓	
Other/Notes					

Order book and poster: unofficialeagleguide.com ©2014 Kent Clizbe

Personal Fitness Merit Badge

12-Week Fitness Program Log

Weekly Fitness Activity Log: Week Number _____

Scout Name: _____   **Date:** _____

Personal Fitness Merit Badge

Order book and poster:
unofficialeagleguide.com
©2014 Kent Clizbe

	Run, Swim, Bike	Exercise name ____	Exercise name ____	Exercise name ____	Heart rate
Distance/Time					
Number of repetitions	▓				▓
Beats per minute before/after	▓	▓	▓	▓	
Other/Notes					

Personal Fitness Merit Badge

12-Week Fitness Program Log

Weekly Fitness Activity Log: Week Number _____

Scout Name: _____   **Date:** _____

Personal Fitness Merit Badge

	Run, Swim, Bike	Exercise name _____	Exercise name _____	Exercise name _____	Heart rate
Distance/Time					
Number of repetitions					
Beats per minute before/after					
Other/Notes					

Order book and poster: unofficialeagleguide.com c2014 Kent Clizbe

Personal Fitness Merit Badge

12-Week Fitness Program Log

Weekly Fitness Activity Log: Week Number _____

Scout Name: _____   **Date:** _____

	Run, Swim, Bike	Exercise name ___	Exercise name ___	Exercise name ___	Heart rate
Dista..ce/Time					
Number of repetitions					
Beats per minute before/after					
Other/Notes					

Personal Fitness Merit Badge

Order book and poster: unofficialeagleguide.com c2014 Kent Clizbe

Personal Fitness Merit Badge

Fitness Test Charts

Post-Program Fitness Test

Scout Name:_____**Date:**_____

Test ⇒	Aerobic Fitness	Flexibility	Strength
Run/Walk Time to complete 1 mile			
Sit-n-reach box **4th reach** distance Hold for 15 sec.			
Sit-ups Number correctly done in 60 sec.			
Pull-ups Number correctly done in 60 sec.			
Push-ups Number correctly done in 60 sec.			

Family Life Merit Badge

90 Day Chore/Duty requirement:

"Prepare a list of your regular home duties or chores (at least five) and do them for 90 days. Keep a record of how often you do each of them."

The next 13 pages are charts you can use for this project. Carefully cut a chart out of the book each week. Put it up on your refrigerator, or on a handy wall. You could put it up next to your **UNOFFICAL Eagle Trail Poster.**

Directions:

1. Each week, note the dates for that week, for example: **March 10-16, 2014** at the top of the chart.

2. Then fill in your chores or duties in the top row. That row might look like this:

Chore/Duty	Dishes	Trash	Feed dog	Mow lawn	Make bed

3. Each day, use the chart to keep track of the chores you do.

4. Start a new chart the next week. Continue this for the 13 weeks required for the Family Life merit badge.

Family Life Merit Badge

90 Day Chore/Duty Charts

Week of: _____ _____ - _____ , 20 ___
(Month)   (Year)

Chore/Duty ⇒	Monday	Tuesday	Wednesday	Thursday	Friday	Saturday	Sunday

Order book and poster: unofficialeagleguide.com c2014 Kent Clizbe

Family Life Merit Badge

90 Day Chore/Duty Charts

Week of: _____ (Month) _____ - _____, 20 ___ (Year)							
Chore/Duty ⟹	Monday	Tuesday	Wednesday	Thursday	Friday	Saturday	Sunday

Order book and poster: unofficialeagleguide.com c2014 Kent Clizbe

Family Life Merit Badge

90 Day Chore/Duty Charts

Week of: _____ (Month) ___ - ___, 20__ (Year)

Chore/Duty ⇒					
Monday					
Tuesday					
Wednesday					
Thursday					
Friday					
Saturday					
Sunday					

Order book and poster:
unofficialeagleguide.com
c2014 Kent Clizbe

Family Life Merit Badge

90 Day Chore/Duty Charts

Week of: _____ (Month) _____ - ____, 20 ___ (Year)							
Chore/Duty ⇒	Monday	Tuesday	Wednesday	Thursday	Friday	Saturday	Sunday

Family Life Merit Badge

90 Day Chore/Duty Charts

Week of: _____ - _____, 20___
(Month)   (Year)

Chore/Duty ⇒	Monday	Tuesday	Wednesday	Thursday	Friday	Saturday	Sunday

Order book and poster:
unofficialeagleguide.com
c2014 Kent Clizbe

Family Life Merit Badge

90 Day Chore/Duty Charts

Week of: _____ (Month) _____ - _____, 20___ (Year)

Chore/Duty ⇒	Monday	Tuesday	Wednesday	Thursday	Friday	Saturday	Sunday

Order book and poster: unofficialeagleguide.com c2014 Kent Clizbe

Family Life Merit Badge

90 Day Chore/Duty Charts

Week of: _____ - _____ , 20 ____
                        (Month)   (Year)

Chore/Duty ⟹					
Monday					
Tuesday					
Wednesday					
Thursday					
Friday					
Saturday					
Sunday					

Order book and poster:
unofficialeagleguide.com
©2014 Kent Clizbe

Family Life Merit Badge

90 Day Chore/Duty Charts

Week of: _____ (Month) - _____, 20____ (Year)

Chore/Duty ⇒	Monday	Tuesday	Wednesday	Thursday	Friday	Saturday	Sunday

Family Life Merit Badge

90 Day Chore/Duty Charts

Week of: _____ (Month) _____ - _____, 20 ___ (Year)

Chore/Duty ⇒	Monday	Tuesday	Wednesday	Thursday	Friday	Saturday	Sunday

Order book and poster:
unofficialeagleguide.com
C2014 Kent Clizbe

Family Life Merit Badge

90 Day Chore/Duty Charts

Week of: _____ (Month) _____ - _____, **20**___ (Year)

Chore/Duty ⟹	Monday	Tuesday	Wednesday	Thursday	Friday	Saturday	Sunday

Order book and poster: unofficialeagleguide.com c2014 Kent Clizbe

Family Life Merit Badge

90 Day Chore/Duty Charts

Week of: _____ - _____, 20 ____

(Month)   (Year)

Chore/Duty ⇒	Monday	Tuesday	Wednesday	Thursday	Friday	Saturday	Sunday

Order book and poster: unofficialeagleguide.com ©2014 Kent Clizbe

Family Life Merit Badge

90 Day Chore/Duty Charts

Week of: _____ (Month) _____ - _____, **20** ___ (Year)

Chore/Duty ⇒	Monday	Tuesday	Wednesday	Thursday	Friday	Saturday	Sunday

Order book and poster:
unofficialeagleguide.com
c2014 Kent Clizbe

Family Life Merit Badge

90 Day Chore/Duty Charts

Week of: _____ (Month) _____ - _____, 20____ (Year)

Chore/Duty ⇒	Monday	Tuesday	Wednesday	Thursday	Friday	Saturday	Sunday

Order book and poster: unofficialeagleguide.com ©2014 Kent Clizbe

Personal Management Merit Badge

Income/Expenses—Budget vs. Actual requirement:

"Prepare a budget reflecting your expected income (allowance, gifts, wages), expenses, and savings."

Directions:

1. Using the Budgeted Amounts side of the Budgeted vs. Actual chart on the following page, estimate your income and expenses.

2. First, estimate your weekly income and expenses. Then, using the weekly amounts, estimate your income and expenses for the next three months.

3. Later, you'll enter your actual income and expenses on the Actual Amounts side. (See the Actual Income and Expenses directions for full details).

Personal Management Merit Badge

Income/Expenses—Budget vs. Actual Chart

Income/Expenses Account-- Budget vs. Actual   Scout Name:

Income Sources	Budgeted Amount					Actual Amounts					Difference Actual- Budgeted
	Weekly	Month 1	Month 2	Month 3	Total	Weekly	Month 1	Month 2	Month 3	Total	
Allowance											
Wages											
Gifts											
Other											
Income Totals											

Expenses	Budgeted Amount					Actual Amounts					
	Weekly	Month 1	Month 2	Month 3	Total	Weekly	Month 1	Month 2	Month 3	Total	
Savings											
Charity											
Food											
Entertainment											
Videos/Music/Games											
Recreation											
Hobbies/Sports											
Travel											
Reading											
Gifts											
Other: _____											

Order book and poster: unofficialeagleguide.com ©2014 Kent Clizbe

Personal Management Merit Badge

Actual Income and Expenses—13 week requirement:

"Track your actual income, expenses, and savings for 13 consecutive weeks. Compare expected income with expected expenses. If expenses exceed income, determine steps to balance your budget. If income exceeds expenses, state how you would use the excess money (new goal, savings). When complete, present the results to your merit badge counselor."

Directions:

4. Using the Actual Income and Expenses charts on the following pages, keep a record of your income and expenses. (Each chart has two weeks on it—first on top, second on bottom.)

5. Each week, total your income and your expenses. Subtract expenses total from income total. Enter this in the last column. If it is negative, or less than zero, put a negative (-) sign next to the number.

6. Each month, add the totals from the weeks that month. Write the monthly actual totals in the Actual Amounts space on the Budget vs. Actual chart.

7. At the end of 13 weeks, total all weeks income and expenses.

8. Look at your Budgeted vs. Actual chart. Compare your budgeted income and expenses to the actual income and expenses.

9. Discuss with your merit badge counselor how you can balance your budget, or your plans for the excess money.

Personal Management Merit Badge

Actual Income and Expenses—13 Consecutive Weeks

Actual Income and Expenses Weeks___ and ___ Scout Name:___			
Description of Item	Income	Expense	Income minus Expenses
Totals--Week ___ (-) if expenses more than income	Income	Expense	Income minus Expenses
Totals--Week ___ (-) if expenses more than income			

Order book and poster:
unofficialeagleguide.com
c2014 Kent Clizbe

Personal Management Merit Badge

Actual Income and Expenses—13 Consecutive Weeks

Actual Income and Expenses Weeks ___ and ___ *Scout Name:* ___	Income	Expense	Income minus Expenses
Description of Item	Income	Expense	Income minus Expenses
Order book and poster: unofficialeagleguide.com c2014 Kent Clizbe			
Totals-Week ___ (-) If expenses more than income			Income minus Expenses
Description of Item	Income	Expense	
Totals-Week ___ (-) If expenses more than income			

Personal Management Merit Badge

Actual Income and Expenses—13 Consecutive Weeks

Actual Income and Expenses Weeks ___ and ___ Scout Name: ___			
Description of Item	Income	Expense	Income minus Expenses
Totals–Week ___			
(–) if expense more than income			
Description of Item	Income	Expense	Income minus Expenses
Totals–Week ___			
(–) if expenses more than income			

Personal Management Merit Badge

Actual Income and Expenses—13 Consecutive Weeks

Actual Income and Expenses Weeks ____ and ____ *Scout Name:* ____			
	Description of Item	Income	Expense	Income minus Expenses
Order book and poster: unofficialeagleguide.com c2014 Kent Clizbe			
Totals–Week ___ (-) If expenses more than income	*Description of Item*	Income	Expense	Income minus Expenses
Totals–Week ___ (-) If expenses more than income			Income minus Expenses

Personal Management Merit Badge

Actual Income and Expenses—13 Consecutive Weeks

Actual Income and Expenses   **Weeks____ and ____**   *Scout Name:* _____

Description of Item	Income	Expense	Income minus Expenses
Totals—Week ____ (-) if expense more than income		Income	Income minus Expenses
Description of Item			
Totals—Week ____ (-) if expense more than income		Expense	Income minus Expenses

Order book and poster:
unofficialeagleguide.com
c2014 Kent Clizbe

Personal Management Merit Badge

Actual Income and Expenses—13 Consecutive Weeks

Actual Income and Expenses Weeks ___ and ___ *Scout Name:* ___			
Description of Item	Income	Expense	Income minus Expenses
Totals–Week ___ (–) If expenses more than income	Description of Item	Income	Expense	Income minus Expenses
Totals–Week ___ (–) If expenses more than income			

Order book and poster:
unofficialeagleguide.com
c2014 Kent Clizbe

Personal Management Merit Badge

Actual Income and Expenses—13 Consecutive Weeks

Actual Income and Expenses   Weeks_____ and ____   Scout Name:_____

Order book and poster:
unofficialeagleguide.com
©2014 Kent Clizbe

Description of Item	Income	Expense	Income minus Expenses

Totals—Week____   (-) if expenses more than income

Description of Item

Income

Expense

Income minus Expenses

Totals—Week____   (-) if expenses more than income

Personal Management Merit Badge

One week Prioritized To Do List requirement:

"Write a "to do" list of tasks or activities, such as homework assignments, chores, and personal projects, that must be done in the coming week. List these in order of importance to you."

Directions:

1. Think of the things you need to do next week.

2. Write each item on its own line in the chart (One Week Prioritized "To Do" List) on the next page.

3. Think of how important to you each item is. The most important item will be number 1.

4. Put the number of each item in the "Priority" column. It should look something like this:

Task To Do	*Priority*
Mow lawn	3
Visit Granpa	1
Weed garden	4
Write thank you notes	2

Personal Management Merit Badge

One Week Prioritized "To Do" List

Task To Do	Priority

Personal Management Merit Badge

One week Planned Activities Schedule requirement:

"Make a seven-day calendar or schedule. Put in your set activities, such as school classes, sports practices or games, jobs or chores, and/or Scout or church or club meetings, then plan when you will do all the tasks from your "to do" list between your set activities."

Directions:

1. Using the Planned Activities Schedule on the next page, enter your regularly scheduled activities (piano lessons, soccer practice, homework, for example). Enter your activities in the right block, for morning (A.M.) or afternoon and evening (P.M.), for each day.

2. Look at your Prioritized To Do List (use the chart on page 139). Enter those activities on your Planned Activities Schedule.

3. Next, you'll use the Actual Activities Log (page 147) to keep track of what you actually do. Later you'll compare your plan with what you actually did.

Personal Management Merit Badge

One Week Planned Activities Schedule

Week of: _____ (Month) _____ - _____, 20 ___ (Year)	A.M.	P.M
Monday		
Tuesday		
Wednesday		
Thursday		
Friday		
Saturday		
Sunday		

Order book and poster:
unofficialeagleguide.com
c2014 Kent Clizbe

Personal Management Merit Badge

One week Actual Activities Log requirement:

"Follow the one-week schedule you planned. Keep a daily diary or journal during each of the seven days of this week's activities, writing down when you completed each of the tasks on your "to do" list compared to when you scheduled them. "

Directions:

1. Use the Actual Activities Log on the next page. Each day, write down what you actually did that day. Maybe your baseball practice was cancelled. Maybe it rained, so you could not mow the lawn, as you had planned. Be sure to enter your activities in the right block, for morning (A.M.) or afternoon and evening (P.M.), for each day.

2. At the end of the week, compare your Actual Activities Log with your Planned Activities Schedule. Think about why some of your planned time slots worked out, and why others might not have worked out. Could you adjust your schedule next time? Be ready to talk to your merit badge counselor about this.

Personal Management Merit Badge

One Week Actual Activities Log

Week of:	Monday	Tuesday	Wednesday	Thursday	Friday	Saturday	Sunday
A.M.							
P.M.							

(Month) _____ - _____, 20____ (Year)

Order book and poster: unofficialeagleguide.com c2014 Kent Clizbe

Camping Merit Badge

20 Nights of Camping Requirement

"Camp a total of at least 20 nights at designated Scouting activities or events. One long-term camping experience of up to six consecutive nights may be applied toward this requirement. Sleep each night under the sky or in a tent you have pitched. If the camp provides a tent that has already been pitched, you need not pitch your own tent."

Directions:

1. Each night you camp out in a Scouting activity or event; enter the details on the log on the next page.

2. Be sure that you check the Camping Merit Badge requirements for details on nights that count for this.

Camping Merit Badge

20 Nights Camping Log

Night Number, Location	Date of Night	Pitch tent, sky, or camp tent?	Notes
1			
2			
3			
4			
5			
6			
7			
8			
9			
10			
11			
12			
13			
14			
15			
16			
17			
18			
19			
20			

UNOFFICIAL EAGLE TRAIL POSTER

Reminder and Motivation Aid for Eagle Trail

You should have this Poster ready the day your Cub Scout becomes a Boy Scout. Use it to remind and motivate your Scout on the Road to Eagle.

As a book buyer you are entitled to a discounted 8x12 inch print of the poster. Forward proof of purchase in an email to:

posterplease@unofficialeagleguide.com

Or to purchase the poster by itself, follow the links at:

www.unofficialeagleguide.com

Directions:

1. Attach your Poster to a convenient place. Put it somewhere that you will see every day. Maybe on your bedroom wall. Or in the bathroom. It should be somewhere that everyone can see easily.

2. Write your name in the space on the bottom left.

3. Beginning at the bottom, you will climb the steps up the chart to the top right—when you earn your Eagle Rank.

4. Study the steps up the chart. This chart helps you to remember each of the steps in the UNOFFICIAL Guide Strategy.

5. The "First Four" Eagle Required Merit badges and their long-term requirements are the first steps.

6. Each time you complete one of the steps, write the date on that level.

7. The next steps are the other major Eagle requirements.

8. Be sure that you follow the Official Eagle Rank requirements, and work with your Scoutmaster.

An 8x12 inch version of this poster is available at:
www.unofficialeagleguide.com

AUTHOR PROFILE

Kent Clizbe has two sons who have earned Eagle—Eli, in 2006; and Isaac in 2013. Kent and his wife, Noli, used Scouting's principles as guideposts in raising their boys. Observing boys raised outside of Scouting, and those raised as Scouts, it was clear to Kent that Scouting is a highly effective man-making program.

Kent's sons both earned full 4 year college scholarships from Army ROTC. Eli served in both Iraq and Afghanistan.

Kent's professional background includes counter-terrorism and counter-intelligence operations in the CIA, executive recruiting, instructional design, teaching English as a Foreign Language, refugee services, and other teaching and consulting work. He served as a linguist in the US Air Force. His education includes an MA and BA in Linguistics, and graduate work in Instructional Design and Business.

He is the author of published and upcoming books on intelligence history, political history, personal health, education, and child-rearing.

Full details are on: *www.kentclizbe.com*

ACKNOWLEDGEMENTS

Many or most of the people who deserve credit have slipped into the mists of memory—faces clear, but names long forgotten. The Cubmaster who spoke at an information session in1994. The volunteers at summer camps, Pinewood Derbies. Den leaders, Cubmasters, Scoutmasters, fellow parents, all of Troop 1154, and more. Not mentioning names doesn't mean their guidance and help was not appreciated—they were crucial.

A few people took precious time to read the drafts, and provide much needed feedback. Ronnie Spence, Chris Mangione, Abdul Rashid Abdullah, Doug Pratt. For Cotillion, the most gracious Jean Ann Michie provided guidance. Any mistakes on any subject are all mine, though.

The most valuable guidance and support came from my family: Noli, Elias and Isaac. They make it all possible.